'I just pray some cartoonist
doesn't come blundering
into this delicate situation'

THE BEST OF

2006

MATTHEW PRITCHETT

studied at St Martin's School of Art in London and first saw himself published in the *New Statesman* during one of its rare lapses from high seriousness. He has been the *Daily Telegraph*'s front-page pocket cartoonist since 1988. In 1995, 1996, 1999 and 2005 he was the winner of the Cartoon Arts Trust Award and in 1991 and 2004 he was 'What the Papers Say' Cartoonist of the Year. In 1996, 1998 and 2000 he was *UK Press Gazette* Cartoonist of the Year and in 2002 he received an MBE.

'If I had to choose, I'd rather
John Prescott punched me...'

The Daily Telegraph

THE BEST OF

MATT

2006

An Orion paperback

First published in Great Britain in 2006 by
Orion Books
A division of the Orion Publishing Group Ltd
Orion House
5 Upper St Martin's Lane
London WC2H 9EA

10 9 8 7 6 5 4 3

A CIP catalogue record for this book
is available from the British Library

ISBN 13 978 07528 8098 3
ISBN 10 0 7528 8098 5

Printed and bound in Great Britain by Butler & Tanner Ltd,
Frome and London

The Orion Publishing Group's policy is to use papers that
are natural, renewable and recyclable products and
made from wood grown in sustainable forests. The logging
and manufacturing processes are expected to conform to
the environmental regulations of the country of origin.

www.orionbooks.co.uk

'What do we want?
Why did we come here?
What were we saying?'

THE BEST OF
MATT
2006

'How free range is the chicken?
Has it ever been to Turkey?'

'This is Britain's bird flu prevention scheme'

'On a more positive note,
I've stopped worrying
about my pension'

'I've done the brown
speckly one...'

'I've got you a tiny bell,
a little mirror and
a box of Trill'

'Another bird is
tormenting our cat'

'Our chef's speciality is
chicken cooked in Lemsip'

'I glorified bird flu'

The Tories

'I put the dog out,
it's terrified of Tory
leadership debates'

'May I recommend this wine;
it's young and untested'

'I'm toying with the idea of
skipping a generation'

Young challenger takes on old guard

The Tories

'By the time it's all over,
David Cameron will
be too old'

'I may recently have apologised
for being a Conservative. I
now realise this was wrong
and I'm very sorry'

Cameron wins – and makes
changes

'I had that nightmare again –
I'm in a room with the shadow
cabinet and I suddenly realise
I'm wearing a tie'

'txt msg 2 tories:
brng bck hngng + flggng'

The Tories

'Let's try a new consensus –
let's both agree you're wrong'

'It's the Tory party that wants
to hear your views, not me'

'It may already be too late to
save Charles Kennedy'

'It looks like a contest between
the Lib Dem big beasts,
Thingummy and Whatsisname'

Lib Dems have their own leadership problems

The Lib Dems

'I'm sorry, sir, I really don't want to keep talking about proportional representation'

Troubles continue …

'It makes you realise how insignificant the Lib Dems are'

Labour

'Water rationing – just at the time John Prescott could do with a cold shower'

Prescott's troubles

'I'm giving your successor
time to bed down'

'Well, Mr Blair was looking
for a lasting legacy...'

When will Blair go?

Labour

Margaret Beckett promoted

Cash for Honours

'If you just "lend" me a biscuit
then nobody need know'

'And I'm leaving £1million
to the Labour Party'

No.10's Humphrey dies

'The problem with teenagers is, they get one A-level and they don't know when to stop'

'And if you pull this lever they give you an A-level'

Dumbing down

'They're from Gordon Brown – millions of A grade GCSEs'

'I want it all – I'm going to wait until after my GCSEs to have a baby'

Educating the world

'The school's rubbish, but he's attending a very good shopping centre'

'When the Germans mess up
an election they do it
very efficiently'

'When you eat spaghetti it
always ends up looking like an
Italian election result'

German and Italian election stalemates

'Shut up about jet lag'

'We heard that you fly
secretly round the world...'

'Could I have one of Zarqawi's grace-and-favour caves?'

Al-Qaida leader shot

'And how well cooked
would you like your car?'

'It's my French homework'

French riots

Foreign Affairs

'We're going for a romantic
weekend in Paris'

'The neighbours have got a
place in France'

French riots

Home Office disaster …

Law and Order

'...The Home Office?...
Very satisfied...'

'Socks are like convicted
foreign criminals – you can
never keep track of them all'

'I thought they'd never leave'

'I'm terribly sorry, I've locked myself out again'

Law and Order

'Don't upset the waiter – I
think he came to this country
by hijacking a plane'

'Sorry I'm late, I had to fight
my way through the crowds
of anti-terror police'

'Life' doesn't mean life

'It's your mother,
she's on the run'

'I've baked you a cake and inside
it I've hidden another cake'

Rebel pensioners

'We've had a tip-off about an illegal retirement party'

'...and the smaller pensioners could go up chimneys...'

'And if you live near an elderly person why not pop in and tell them to get a job'

'We've got something put
aside for you for a rainy day'

'It's not just my home,
it's my pension as well'

Health

'We're going to have to let you go'

'I felt unwell while I was at the job centre. Luckily it was full of NHS staff'

'...bag...gun...bullets...'

'When you said you'd bought a nurse's outfit...'

'Is your body actually two write-offs welded together?'

'A box of cornflakes? Do you have an appointment?'

'...And by the time you come round, the hospital will have closed down'

'Let me through, I'm a 12-year-old boy'

IT failures

24-hour drinking

'Walking the dog? You're just sneaking out to go home!'

'I know what you're thinking
and you're right – this is all
Tessa Jowell's fault'

'I must phone my children –
will you tell me when it's
Christmas day?'

'Two small boys offered to wash my car and then ran off with my bucket of water'

'Am I allowed to use my
hosepipe to pump rainwater
out of the house?'

'To hell with it, when we get
home I'm going to flush the loo'

'We've run out of
"Don't Panic Buy" notices'

'I've half a mind
to buy a car'

Petrol

'I'm just looking, thank you'

'And this one has uninterrupted views over Kent'

'I don't object to the housing development but NOBODY calls me middle-class'

Nimby

'The Old Kent Road with two brothels, you owe...'

'Thank goodness you stopped that wind farm being built'

The Church

'Women should be allowed
to become bishops – but not at
weekends or peak times'

Britishness

'If they integrated into society
and stopped mixing only
with each other, they
wouldn't feel so isolated'

'Making a cake for the
church fete is not the same
as "becoming radicalised"'

'I got an "A" in British Values –
I said the homework infringed
my human rights'

The Ashes

'Bite your own nails'

'No, I meant is there any news about the cricket?'

'Stop smiling, you're
upsetting the dog'

'HOWZAT?'

'I'm moving to Heathrow airport – they have a slower pace of life over there'

'Finish your supper – there are people on BA flights who'd be glad of that'

'Nice card from Prince Philip'

'You knew the bad weather was coming; you should have had a sarcastic remark prepared'

The World Cup

'You could at least
WATCH the England matches'

'It's on. Start watering'

'If anyone here present knows of the score in the England–Portugal match, let him speak now'

England go out ... and Zidane butts off.

And finally …

'I slipped ten of the new weight-loss pills into his supper and he simply vanished'

'The Bordeaux? We do it in bottles, carafes, or lakes…'

'Martini, shaken not stirred'

The MI6 rock

'A high golf handicap does
not make you eligible for
incapacity benefit'

And finally …

'If Mr Cameron wants to
come and watch,
I'm defrosting my fridge'

Environmentally friendly
Cameron

'It looked like Santa's grotto –
how was I meant to know it
was a gay wedding'

And finally . . .

'When you said my husband would be a guinea pig...'

'I will now run this bath without the aid of a thermostat'

Health and safety gone mad

And finally ...

'Let's run away to England and have a cigarette'

'Think of all the happy times...well, think of the car-sharing lane'

'What on earth are you doing?
Do you realise how much
a TV licence costs?'

And finally …

'I attend as many parenting classes as I can – anything to get away from my children'

'I think I've had enough'

Whale sails up the Thames

'Blenkinsop, I think we've found the last breeding pair...'

And finally …

'I'm terribly sorry,
Sir Freddie Laker, we seem
to have lost your luggage'

'It's only your tiny salary
that keeps us together'

'You can always tell the females – they have the smaller salaries'

'Forty million lottery scratchcards, please'

And finally …

'WHY WOULD I BE INTERESTED IN THAT?'

'My mum's older than your mum'

Pensioner Mum

'I feel like I've been stabbed in the back'

'I think she's seen the reviews of the film'

The Da Vinci Code

And finally …